A Foreign Landscape

Soos

Other books you may enjoy
from Realities Library:

| | |
|---|---|
| Searching The Shadows | Ella Blanche |
| Reaching In Silence | Kay Closson |
| The Devil Sang In Tune | Andonis Fostieris |
| Far From The Garden | Don MacQueen |

Realities Library
a non-profit corporation
2745 Monterey Hwy #76
San Jose, CA 95111



Copyright 1984 by Realities Library
ISBN 0-916982-31-9
LC# 84-060368

A Foreign Landscape

for two of my eternal sirens:
A Fajilan
Paraskevi

Vinum daemonum

My embroidered grammar is
kneaded into loaves that sit
to rise in the morning sunlight.
The dough is patient and changes
shape by noon, vaguely resembling
its past incarnation of dizzying
language spilled from an
enclosure which houses ink
and guages the ink with
some precision.

The heart through your eyes

Beneath the sea there is a glass
with painted models singing in the aether.
A porcelain dancer, tapped gently,
calls forth in the proper key.
The wine has been swallowed by the silent coral.
The strings of my lute remain taut although
the glues have softened to the point where
the tunes can be played only with my breath.

Pass through this moment
as a traveler
reaching for a steady
aspiration,
seeking the positive
knowledge that an
entire moment is
vivid in its
intense infinity.

Birth of discovery

Each dream is a voyage
along an intricate chemistry —
generating voltages of mystery.

Patience is required
to spend silent moments
studying your shadows.

Among the reeds of a great
river, I search for
your presence.

You are contained in the wind.

Patience is required
to run across the darkness
with accurate footsteps.

At the horizon I shout,
"Push aside the light!
Let me enter the moment!"

Patience is required
to master the precise
choreography

which unveils the soul.

Undisciplined reflection

The surface wades below motions,
    dark with rolling restraint.

    Sprawled under himself,
    she is opening in composite rhythm
    music brushed out of diagonal petals.
    The dance links blossoms to petals.
    The sea shapes an action worn with desire
        out of fragments.

We become silence.
One is one are each other.

Silence cannot speak the dark sleep.

Identical understanding methods
    have always been adopted to know,
    to attempt to understand commonplace.
    Perspective will determine justice.

When anything figures nervous,
think every statement used the thought.
Trust sounds.

Being probably myself,
I am actually more rational
    than terrible.

Meaning is experience in segments.

The sun wants the surf visible to the world.

Counting footsteps

In the distance you turn
hypnotized by the latitude.

The slope is gentle
but divulges in a flame
of sunlight — your eyes
gleaming in the soundless
movement of a star.

You are now walking this way
and stand for a brief moment
savagely delicate
and glow at the particular
perfect distance of passion.

Obscure reveries

The latitude of the sun blows smoke through twisted leaves.
An evening knowledge whispers a soft spray
toward your gold braided skirt.
The olive tree of California breeds air
from the Mediterranean in the moonlight.
A poem read in the mist of a light rainfall
is moved with silent powers through a foreign landscape.
Your industry is destined to be cemented with the clouds,
roughly cracked between your breasts. A chosen
fruit has taken wing, cooling in the atmosphere
and not bothering to return in sleep.
To lengthen a season, language must exist
in a powerful sphere of trust.

and not bothering to return in sleep.
A trembling candlelight blinks through the incense as
you whirl with an accurate innocence through the clouds
of this fossiled hemisphere. To lengthen a season,
language must exist in a powerful sphere of trust.

l'amour est l'enfant de la liberte

A shadow trembles on your garments
while thick incense perfumes the air
between your eyes and a single candle.
A flowered moon with bandit spurs
rides a giant horse through the
backwater aroma of the stars.
Water echoes the rocking reverberations
of constellations wounded by ancient souls.
Through muddy atmospheres daylight
tastes the salt of weeping molecules.
A sealed rose bud wrestles anxious
violins blurring the emptiness of a single atom.
You shall cross a bridge of circles
and face the magic fruit of a fable
pulsing through my tranquil bloodstream
and dream the diagrams of my words.

A trusting voyage

The earth descends on its wobbling axis
spinning ever slower while people are singing
in the dark temples of the city.
Magic is imposed through the eyes of space.
Tribes of men invade the light of the solar system
with minds set on alchemy, pulling themselves
through an invention of swallowed gravity.
The light will not escape, but falls back
upon itself in a mock burial of galaxies.
The imagined holes are eyes of other universes
peering at swirling minor stars.
A natural visionary wrestles the singing gypsy
for a seat on the stream.
The path circles small perfections
entering the bones of neutrinos
as well as the spaces between heartbeats.
A song created while hanging on the webs
between the stars opens on coastal harbors.
The earth discards uniform directions.
Magic will barter for protective asylum.
The elders of all tribes soar in drunken
fellowship on the bearings of the stars.

The passion of flight

Your eyelids grope the air for the passion of flight
as distant dawn dries the dew off stones.
Not more than this I ask: let me watch
you vanish through the flute of atmosphere.
The shell surrounding my soul has disappeared
but I will not allow the rippling breezes
of my heart to threaten your silence and
the images of your eyes through the clouds.
When you reach the moon or the sun
I will send a bird to quell the dances
of any tempest which may break a wing.

Your frozen music

a skeleton weight hammers underground.
an ordinary whisper breathes visions
at the feet of morning burials,
pure in the galaxy of nightmares.
in bodies weighted by heat,
priests embrace entrances to love.
removing time leaves spoken words
that aren't blind in the coolest muscles.
each scale passes natural harmonies
on a path deeper than tortured sanctuaries.
an immeasurable daughter crawls
toward your forgotten expressions,
translating your frozen music.
my hands invade the paradox
with a warm guitar. singing.
voices listen.

True touch

Your touch is not physical.
Your dreams fly higher than Icarus.
But wings no longer melt.
Except in hearts.
Hearts melt near light.
A single breath warms many weeks.
Your beauty sleeps in castles miles away.
We are aware of dreams.
A dream does not become a dream.
Until it is over.
Daily bread is blessed.
Daily prayer is received.
I sing for you daily.
I sing a song of true touch from your fingers.
Touch me.
Touch you.
Touch the life of places we visit without touch.

The dissonance of love

The sun corrected your reflection
and reversed the radiant satisfaction
achieved by disturbed experience.
The strongest tides pull clouds through the open skies
and venture untravelled waters through hidden experience
in the depth of thick salt. Eager luminosity
speaks through your visible desires,
surfacing with an anxious brilliance.
My mind is greedy for light.
There is essence in the dissonance of love.
Examine the thresholds you stumble upon.
Hold the flame of your thoughts
among the pleasure of confident worlds.
Satisfy all budding comparisons with a simple intensity.
The sun is threading my attention.
A precious harmony answers your melting passion
and names the words of love by number.

Wine

I paint deep eyes on the white canvas.
They collapse in determined melodic chants
and hunt the song of uncommon shadows
while I draw in the belly, shoulders and hair.
The stomach pulses with laughter
and the shoulders dance.
The hair unwinds and becomes difficult
because the eyes begin to dazzle.
The painting begins to watch my nervous
trembling as I reach for more drink.
The feet are no different than the softness
of other painted feet,
yet they pace the floor, giggling madly.
The clothing I paint loose.
This painting is left undone.
I will not watch the lips and fingers blossom
their own knowledge. I cannot.
I sweep the studio clean
and go home to finish the bottle.
Tomorrow I'll buy a new canvas.

Triad

Elaborate on the circuit of undecipherable gestures,
the divine nature of chaos.
Two perfect hydrogen atoms invade a singular space.
One electron becomes excited and enters the sphere
of a once perfect entity creating
one negative isotope and one positive isotope.
An isotope is not a stable atom.
Clinging to graditude and gentleness,
we can mirror incoherent ciphers.
There are variations of satisfaction,
circular distances, impatient universes,
faceless dreamers, and many consecrated hallucinations.
They are there. Obstinately dragging the beginning
of all immediate reflections through the mud.
The misplaced electron becomes a carnival
condemned to seek the suburb of a soul
until one of its personal permutations discovers
a domicile for its own particular thirst.
If it rears back to the original atom of escape,
it is bounced back to oblivion for lack of space.
It has placed itself in an improvisitory cosmos,
imprisoned in the labyrinth of its own awareness.
If that electron is accepted by the nucleus of the atom
it made into a negative isotope, then another electron
becomes a wild persian horse invading the functioning
restlessness of the billions of electrical spheres
influencing traditional affections.

Strong toil of grace

From behind the tree you dance
with the grasshoppers
in a precise condition of clarity.
Suns whirl in the backround.
The ballet slippers
summon your feet with elaborate powers;
experienced testaments wandering
the hems of woolen shadows.
In a mirror through the forest
candles blaze atop boulders
and glaciers snag the leaves
at their edges, burning them
with a flowing chill. You dance
higher on the horizon
holding a warmth toward me. I cup
my fingers in thirst and drink
from a river blazing with ships spread
along the further edges. Your feet
touch the tops of sails and spring
aloft around suns saulting in the spray
from the melting glacier.
There is no space between us.
Flesh is a membrane filled with a current
of pure light swimming through
the dances of the boats along the river.
The grasshoppers crowd me with song
when I roll through the spines of dead leaves
searching for sleep. You dance with the warm
music, higher with each twirl and leap.

Dawn

A morning embrace
grows with the decisive fantasy
of uninterrupted intimacy
        (a firm intrusion in the birth
         of a charade of despair)
        (a sleep deeply blessed
         in the future).
The exile of the soul surrounds
the ridges of the heart
exposed in a victorious release.
Lips lean on unintentional instinct,
brushing together as leaves
in a forest
carefully covering skin.
The shapes of mouths
push through the leaves
and reach for each other with bold virtue
and respectable sacrifice.

Gypsy woman

He has left his visions to visit your realm.
The formal prophet of careful order drifts
unnoticed through faithful languages.
He watches you leap into flames and shine
in the quivering tongues of light.
He kindles his strength with rhythm
sprung from the vigorous music
of the wanderers, minstrels, and workers
traveling near your tempered fevers
and tightly woven hymns. You are
the queen of the fire, singing your blessings
to the men who seek peace in their lifetime,
the men prophesizing the weeds
that will be food for mankind and floods
that will provide water. There is nourishment
for life. He is hiding in a shadow. You
watch for his eyes to open.
He is the life of your vision.

Embracing infatuation

Twisting the mind of the twisted with dark mythology
and a discourse on docile love, the gypsy sings
the mystical revelations of an undulating rhythm
taking root in concealed magic. Swaying in
the salvation of song, the gypsy chants the
primeval struggle between eros and agape.
The roadway cradles a power and expanse
of conscious existence, vast in a language
embracing infatuation. This dull emotion sparkles
with broken wine bottles thrown by the gypsy
after fervent conquests of sacred altars.
The gypsy curses the heart and the secret caverns
which lie overly enchanted with majestic dreams.
The gypsy sings of freedom from meditation.

Passion

Hanging from a tree, fruit ripens in specified seasons.
The stones inside moisten, but may be dried for rebirth.
Friendship holds it's liberty and flows over smooth stones
in the hearts of the connoisseurs of metamorphosis and love.

Footsteps burn in the realm of my sleep.
You walk toward me, I pass through and beyond myself
surveying the arrival of each abyss in the memory.
A splendid mist envelops you.
You are rising from the sleeping form.
The mist reaches past me skillfully.
There is only the memory, the strength of failing light.
We fly through many borders, a single wing between us.
After this excursion through veiled theatres of solitude
a passageway to the body opens to receive
and you pass with me, continuing outward through the eyes.
My body quakes, arms reaching for your departing form.

Your dark eyes blaze
in rhythm with a wild marriage
                a dark horizon
                a heart beyond the voices of love.

Conserving embraces

Your cheeks magnify a submissive madness
modulating through joy and laughter.
I translate the music of those moments,
the mirrors of mountains,
the tenderness of confusion
and the secure gestures of life.

The waves follow the shoreline.
Each hour new statues appear as the line recedes.
We look into each other's eyes whispering visions
while dancing upon fresh seaweed.
The tide returns and washes our feet.
A seduction is invented for the paradise of stars.

The lines of centuries are not drawn by minutes.
Beauty that comes from freedom cannot be captured.
The melody may become a dirge for primal lament.
The tomb of the wind may be opened for a common sadness —
    developed by the searing of love.

Looking for a raindrop

I have directed sadness through infinity and emerged
with a new bravery. High in my breast I love you.
   My nakedness is an illusion.
   I harbor my impatience in the mildew of heaven.
   Redemption is gained by crossing a perished bridge.
Nourish your lips with cold water.
Let your eyes enter the wind and transcend the seasons.
Your shadow clouds the inhabitants of its light.
   A persistant resonance sings of your joy
   and your flight through a fragile wooden flute.
   The strains reach my breath and I become
   my own passion, a lunatic dream of myself.

The backrounds

I visited the backrounds of Leonardo
but could not find you there.
The caves had a mysterious light
from within. I walked toward the glow
of the center of the womb. The virgin
on the rocks remained silently content.
A lamp of my conscience shone an obliging
eternity on the glorious festive existence
of vapor. The bridges and roads behind monna
were an eternal day long trip, deep into
the sfumato and birth, celebrated by well traveled
passion and thirst for unrehearsed secrets.

The deep chaos you breath in becomes
a myth through beautiful footsteps
placed neatly on the wind,
bellowing your spirited laughter and
hoarse tears through my studied loneliness.

On the bridge I pause and look out
beyond la Gioconda's left shoulder and
watch you prancing, the perfect coquette.
I find myself not unwillingly pulled
into the intrepid tease, though I see
the pale faces of your followers staring sadly
into a distant rock on the wood panel of the virgin.
I turn aside and complete my walk.

Plankton

You visit the sea with your lover
and I watch you ascend this side of the mountain.
When your small car reaches the peak,
your descent goes unobserved.
The mountain has come between us.
My place is the sea, yet today I attend earth.

>Resolution of the final script
>evolves. A moment is not the
>zygote of time in the heart of
>Artemis. It is a gentle entity.

Lovers create a perfect poetry of the beach
as the tide cools the whiskers of their thighs.
The plankton wades without control
of its movements, in the manner of my
guitar strings and the fibers ripping
from my heart.

A secret marriage

The moonlight cracked the mountain
through the curtains and mist.
A silent silver invades the darkness
in this room, ignoring the heavy heart.
A eunuch emerges from the
shadows and dances for me while
singing the translucent passion
of a secret marriage. I am
not startled when he melts and
freezes over, a eunuch's body
is not threaded to a dream.
I have the freedom to contemplate visions
but choose to spot a single molecule
from your smile and hold it dear
to my burning lump of brain.
The incense strangles the moonlight
and invites this midnight again,
a misty curtain of darkness.

Pathways

I bravely shook hands,
never trembling,
with your lover.
I cannot wash his smell from me.
This jealousy cannot be explained.
Your hand on his body told many stories.
The grace of a body of a working man
is enviable in the eyes of a thin poet
with a broken body leftover from war.
I cannot wash his smell from me.
My mind has been visiting the past.
My clothes are leftovers from the past.
My legs are leftovers from the past.
The pounding temple and bleeding stomach
are leftovers from the past.
The bone in my temple was split
moments after the bones in my legs.
I sometimes dance now,
sometimes walk like a cripple.
It is not easy to remember the war.
I am reminded each day is a war.
I am born in the pathways of wars.
I cannot wash his smell from me.
Meeting your lover tonight,
I was a brave soldier.

Intoxicated with shadows

I

Is there pride in the final acceptance
of death, or simply a short breath
of air between yellowing teeth?

II

I coil and spit venom at my dreams.
I recoil for further attack on my soul.
Before recoiling for a third time, I eat
my entrails, kidneys, and lungs
for breakfast. I will sleep soundless
with a belly full of myself.

III

The feet of the man twitch in odd
spasms as the blood pulses from
the scars deep in his body.
The man whose brain has stationed
itself heavy above his eyelids.

IV

You pick his body from beneath
the flowering bushes of the city gardens.
You search months for his identity
before forgetting his existence.

Humanity

The soul of a beast climaxes
beyond the memory of superstitions.
There are earths for reasons we cannot
(de)  (pro)  scribe.

A hopeful young man
opens the door for the first time,
repeating the history of his race.
There is a certain faith
contained in the power of steadfast myths,
escaping the centuries of fragile waters.

A beast  (gr)  (m)  oans
without humility below ambiguous bridges.
Expected conversations appear
in the beautiful labor of a curious fool
touching the slender thighs of a rude lover,
rough with the shame of a dreaming lion.

The stories of the gods
are  (po)  (squa)  ndered
by the  (bes)  (celes)  tial
dreams of Dionysus.

The waves

Called toward the stone shoreline
the lovers challenge the whispers of impatient daggers.
Their voices covet the duel, wind to shoreline,
armies to texts from ancient fragments
alien to poetry. They manifest the fire of eternity,
the seperation of the mirror from its image,
the focus of the violence of the centuries
originating stone. Near shore they see below the surface.
Nearer the rocks, the sacred depth of black memory.
Above the storm prostrates an unspoken splendor of light.

Their blurred staring wanders between themselves.
A reflected choir invokes the glow of humility.
She strolls through reflections a thousand miles away.

Where can we find two better hemispheres?

Of course I can say simply "I love you".
I can stand before you naked and alive.
I can draw your lips toward me and kiss them forever.
I can whisper the admiration I have for you in your ear.
I can sing the wonder of your hair and your eyes.
I can stand on my fingers and play a pure fool.
I can call to your mother, your father, and your brother
    across the oceans and tell them I love you.
I can talk to your uncle, your aunt, and your nephew
    across the silent night and tell them I love you.
I can bump into your boyfriend and tell him I love you.

This is all so easy. Simple words say I love you.
The words are so easy. So simple. So free.
I love you. I love you. I love you forever.

I cannot go through with it.
It does not erase you from my mind.
I shout at the thunderbolt with unmerciful voice.
My words become magnets which consecrate blood.
I live with the images and draw power from them.
A love is not easily cultivated and seldom ripens
    to a lifetime of nourishment and freedom.

I do not choose words for lovers to struggle with.
I aim for a trajectory of sincerity.
Of course I can say simply "I love you".

The flight of remembered dreams
  —paging through the wedding album

Humble hearts encircle fading smiles in dark snapshots
and you abandon the scene with your arms
anciently surrounding the chains of the plots,
the memories of a love somehow fading without harm.
A strength is garnered from the field of backround
below the gloss of two dimensional life between waxed pages.
Concentrate the color wash that ready lovers crowned
with expectation. Form love as the empty fragment rages
through the inevitable proudness sequenced on daily stages.
Everything moves fast through boredom. A distant sound
moves slowly through the night and oversteps the charms
of correct youthfulness. Hearts are landing in empty lots.

contents




thanks to the editors of common streets, dog river
review, postpoetry, ptolemy and tandava